The Ox Knows Its Owner

Isaiah 1:3

For New Christians and Those in Backslidden State

Christy Tola

ISBN: 978-972924094-2

Unless otherwise indicated all Scriptures
Quotations are taken from the New King James
Version of the Bible.

Part of the Proceeds Will Go Towards
Talent Awareness Program for Youth &
Unemployed Graduates.

(Ox Picture Courtesy freeimages.com)

Christy Tola Arts & Books
P O Box 4243
Oak Park
IL 60304. USA.

Table of Contents

Contact Details 51

IMPORTANT FIRST!

Is Your Soul Saved?

If you have not invited Jesus Christ as your Lord and Savior, this is the time to do so. This is because you need the help of the Holy Spirit. He is our Guide and Comforter in life. He can only come to you after you have invited Jesus Christ, and when you begin to Study the Scriptures, praise, and worship God. You also need Him to help you to pray.

"...If you confess with your mouth the Lord Jesus and believe in your heart that God has raised Him from the dead, you will be saved. For with the heart one believes unto righteousness, and with the mouth confession is made unto salvation" Romans 10:9-10.

Please say the Prayer below:

Dear Heavenly Father, I am sorry for my sins. Please forgive me. Jesus Christ, please come into my life and help me. In Your name I pray. Amen.

It is important that you follow these Instructions:

Prayer

Pray every morning and ask God to protect and order your steps throughout the day. Also, ask the Holy Spirit to reveal your Divine Purpose to you. As you do, He will begin to order your steps and lead you to where you are supposed to be in life.

Read the Bible and Worship
It's important that you create time for your Daily Devotion with God. When you're about to start your Daily Devotion (twice daily is advised), saying the Scripture below will help you. Also, pray and ask the Holy Spirit to teach you, as you study:

"...He opened their understanding,
that they might comprehend the Scriptures" Luke 24:45.

As soon as you become a Christians, you are like a new born baby that requires milk. Likewise, our Souls require spiritual nourishments for it to develop. Therefore, reading the Bible and Praise and Worshipping God will provide the spiritual nourishments that your Soul requires. It will also protect you from 'spiritual infections', ease your pains if you are spiritually afflicted, as well as allow the Holy Spirit to come close and help you.

It's very important that you read the Bible every day but must be accompanied by Gospel Praise and Worship

Music, or songs of adoration to God. This will draw the Holy Spirit to your situation quicker. I will advise you to incorporate reading the Book of Psalms during your Daily Devotion.

Reading the Bible generously will also help you to discern spiritual truth about your life and situations.

> *"I have more understanding than all my teachers,*
> *For Your testimonies are my meditation.*
> *I understand more than the ancients,*
> *Because I keep Your precepts"* Psalm 119:99-100.

As you study, get use to writing Scriptures on small/index cards to meditate on, memorize, and confess, during the day. This will help to protect your mind and strengthen you against temptations.

Go to Church and Fellowship
We are commanded to fellowship with other Christians. But it's important to ask the Holy Spirit to lead you to a Church.

> *"...Let us consider one another in order to stir up love and*
> *good works, not forsaking the assembling of ourselves*
> *together, as is the manner of some, but exhorting one*
> *another"* Hebrews 10:24-25.

One of the major reasons for going to Church is because Corporate Anointing is sometimes required for certain breakthroughs and this is only possible in a church environment. You need the prayers of other Christians and the Pastor. (The Bible says, *One person will chase a thousand and two are capable of putting ten thousand to flight;* Deuteronomy 32:30).

Secondly, the Church is the Holy Spirit School and Classroom. This is where He teaches us, His Students. The Pastors/Ministers are His Mouthpiece. You need a good and experienced Pastor that has been trained by the Holy Spirit, especially if you perceive that you have a major mission to accomplish in life. God will use the Pastor of the Church to train you for your future Ministry or Divine Calling for your life. Therefore, it's important that you pray and ask the Holy Spirit to direct you to His choice of Church for you.

Baptism
Get baptized in your local church. Christians are commanded to do so in the Bible;

"...Let every one of you be baptized in the name of Jesus Christ for the remission of sins; and you shall receive the gift of the Holy Spirit" Acts 2:38.

Serve

As soon as you begin to attend your new Church, volunteer yourself as a worker in any of the Ministries. Also, pray for guidance to serve in the area of ministry that will be of great benefit to your future.

Ask for Guidance

It's also important to always ask the Holy Spirit to guide you in everything that you do, so that He can help you to prevent mistakes. You are permitting Him to help you if you ask. God is the Owner of our lives and the Earth that we live in. We will be operating in the dark if we do not pray or acknowledge Him in all our ways, we are likely to make some mistakes, which are preventable.

> *"The earth is the LORD's, and all its fullness,*
> *The world and those who dwell therein"*
> Psalm 24:1.

> *"In all your ways acknowledge Him,*
> *And He shall direct your paths"*
> Proverbs 3:6.

Love One Another

Love people as we are commanded and try your best to avoid malice and unforgiveness, so your prayers are not hindered. Use Isaiah 40:29 to pray for help if you're struggling in this area.

"A new commandment I give to you, that you love one another; as I have loved you, that you also love one another. By this all will know that you are My disciples, if you have love for one another" John 13:34-35.

Please remember to share the Gospel with your relatives and friends.

God bless you.

Introduction

'The Ox Knows Its Owner' (Isaiah 1:3) is a follow-up Guide prepared to enlighten new Christians and those in backslidden state, the importance of reading the Bible, Praise, Worship, and Prayers, after they have accepted Jesus Christ as their Lord and Savior. It also highlights the importance of keeping up our relationship with God as we continuously abide in Him, as Jesus Christ has commanded, which will prevent us from going back to our old ways of life.

"Abide in Me, and I in you. As the branch cannot bear fruit of itself, unless it abides in the vine, neither can you, unless you abide in Me"
John 15:4.

A consistent Daily Devotion is required to continuously abide in God.

I will employ you to read and think about the Scripture below for a moment, and how it relates to us as Christians;

"The Ox knows its Owner

And the donkey its Master's crib..." Isaiah 1:3.

Once you have given your life to Jesus Christ, then you have come 'home' because He is the Link between Man and God. Therefore, it's important that you stay close to God, so that you can be fed, nourished, and protected.

This book is an eye opener to some fundamentals of Christianity. It's my prayer that every page blesses the Reader. May the eyes of your understanding be opened as you read.

God bless you richly.

Christy Tola.

1

Your New Responsibilities

*"The Ox knows its Owner
And the donkey its Master's crib"*
Isaiah 1:3.

Oxen are used in the olden days to carry loads for their masters. They are purchased and used by their owners as often as they are needed. When we relate this to Christianity, we are also 'purchased' through the Blood of Jesus Christ as soon as we accept Him as our Lord and Savior. He has redeemed us for God, therefore, we are to stay close and be ready to be used for the work of God.

"....With His own blood He entered the Most Holy Place once for all, having obtained eternal redemption" Hebrews 9:12.

Let's take a closer look at the word, *'knows'* from the phrase, *"The Ox knows its Owner..."*

This implies that the Ox is well acquainted with its owner because they are together most of the time. The same should apply to us Christians too. Once we are reconnected back to God through Jesus Christ, we are to begin to seek and stay close to our Creator all the time. This is how we will know Him better, through our relationship with Him.

"Abide in Me, and I in you. As the branch cannot bear fruit of itself, unless it abides in the vine, neither can you, unless you abide in Me" John 15:4.

How can this be achieved? By deliberately creating time to study the Bible, Praise, Worship and pray to God on a daily basis. To know someone is to spend some time with the person. I will suggest that you wake up fifteen to thirty minutes earlier than your normal waking-up time for your Daily Devotion. As said earlier, consistency is also of great importance with your Daily Devotion.

2

Why We Need to Stay Connected

"The Ox knows its Owner
And the donkey its Master's crib"
Isaiah 1:3.

Why should we stay connected to God? We need to stay connected so that we can be:

- o Nourished
- o Protected
- o Be under His guidance
- o For the propagation of the Gospel
- o And be Spiritually Cleansed (when we sin)

Let's briefly look at each of the above listed points.

Spiritual Nourishment

When we read the Scriptures and worship God dedicatedly, we are not only spiritually cleansed, but also nourished and filled with His Anointing. The nourishment helps to fill any void that may have been created in our lives. This is also the time that we are 'repaired', in case we have spiritual injuries. But when we engage ourselves in some of the acts of flesh listed in Galatians 5:19-21 (see 'Spiritual Cleansing' below), the Anointing around us will be affected. That is, any sinful action will make God's Presence to leave temporarily until we repent, read the Scriptures and worship again.

Therefore, it's important that we read the Scriptures and worship God at least twice daily, which will help us to be replenished again. This is similar to when we spray some cologne in the morning and having to re-apply it later in the day. Also, all that God has deposited in us when we are being created will be revealed, when we start to study the Scriptures and worship God all the time.

We Need God's Protection

When we read the Scriptures and praise and worship God, His Anointing stays around us. This is to prevent unclean spirits from entering our lives to cause problems. Their presence can affect and rob us of many important things. Therefore, it's important that we stay away from sinful acts, keep our Bible study and praise and worship consistent, and be careful in all our dealings.

We Need God's Guidance

Proverbs 3 Verse 6 says,

"In all your ways acknowledge Him,
And He shall direct your paths."

We need God's guidance anytime we want to make a major decision or take an important step in our life. It's important that you speak to God about issues concerning your life. Remember that He is our Creator and knows everything about our lives. You cannot navigate this World successfully without the guidance of the Holy Spirit. Only Him knows where all things are in the World-this include things pertaining to your life. You need His directions regarding your Divine Purpose, Divine Location, Life Partner, and more.

Propagation of the Gospel

Let's look at the second line of our key Scripture;

"...And the donkey its Master's crib."

As earlier said, there were no cars and other forms of transportation in the olden days as we currently have and are enjoying today. Back then, one major means of transportation was the use of oxen and donkeys to transport people and goods from one place to another.

God cannot do anything on Earth without the help of us Christians that has been redeemed through Jesus Christ to His Kingdom. We are God's 'Vehicles' and His Spirit flows through us to reach the lost Souls.

We have been commissioned to preach the Gospel. Those that are called to do the work of evangelist or shepherding are His vehicles, as well as those that are not 'officially' called. Therefore, we all have the responsibility to reach out to our family and friends.

"... As the Father has sent Me, I also send you"
John 20:21.

Always remember this: since the ox was bought for its master's use, similarly, we are purchased and redeemed to be used for God's purposes. Therefore, you need to find out what you are supposed to do specifically for God's Kingdom during your prayers. As you ask, God will begin to steer your life in the right direction. Also, when you begin to serve Him dedicatedly, as well as doing all that you are required to do, He will make sure that all your needs are met because you have become one of His 'Employees'.

Spiritual Cleansing

Many times we engage ourselves in some of the things listed in Galatians 5:19-21, which can make us to be spiritually unclean;

"Now the works of the flesh are evident, which are: adultery, fornication, uncleanness, lewdness, idolatry, sorcery, hatred, contentions, jealousies, outbursts of wrath, selfish ambitions, dissensions, heresies, envy, murders, drunkenness, revelries, and the like..."

Also, some of what are being presented in the media can affect and prevent the Presence of God from being around us. For example, ritual-based programs and those with violent contents. Therefore, staying connected through reading of the Scriptures, Praise, Worship, and Prayers, will help us to be spiritually clean, so that God's Presence can be around us to protect us and our stuff.

3

The Process of Fruit Bearing

It's important to know that; when we bear fruit as a Christian, we are productive, and this is our mark of identification with God the Father. Our God is productive and if we are productive as Him, then we are like Him and we look like 'Daddy'!

"By this My Father is glorified, that you bear much fruit; so you will be My disciples" John 15:8.

The Scriptures are Seed and when we study them, they are sown into our lives. Also, when we praise and worship God, the Seed that are sown are then 'watered', which will make the Seed of the Word to grow and help to bud all our hidden talents and divine purpose in life.

Important Information:

Whenever you read the Bible, you are planting some of God's Anointing into your life. This is because the Scriptures are Anointed Words. This means that you are transferring God's blessings, riches, longevity, money, divine health, favor, and many more of what God has, into your life.

After some time (if you're consistent with your Daily Devotion), the Seed will start to grow, and those areas of your life that were once 'dry', will become alive. You will then begin to see changes in every area of your life for everyone to see. Those who used to look down on you and think that you cannot amount to anything in life will now begin to glorify God when they see the incredible changes that has taken place, and the physical evidence of the things that your life has produced. Now you have a testimony!

The Fruit Bearing Christian

Let's look at this illustration; just as trees have many branches, Christ is also a 'Tree', with many Branches. When we give our life to Jesus Christ, we become a Branch according to the Scriptures.

"I am the vine, you are the branches. He who abides in Me, and I in him, bears much fruit; for without Me you can do nothing" John 15:5.

Every tree must bear fruit through its branches. If you, the branch of Christ, are not bearing fruit, then you are spiritually disconnected from God. You must begin to do something about this as soon as this truth is revealed to you. Begin to study the Scriptures, praise, worship, and pray daily, and this must be consistent. Also, of great importance is walking in love which ties everything together.

There must be an evidence of some changes after you've given your life to Jesus Christ. For example, things like good moral character, respect for adults, good health, improvement in your general outlook, and attitude to spiritual things, are all indications that you have continued to stay connected to your Source.

Note this:
If there are unhealthy branches on a tree, the owner of the tree usually removes them. God the Father is our Owner and He's responsible for looking after us and pruning us continuously. The Scripture below illustrates this point;

"I am the true vine, and My Father is the vinedresser. Every branch in Me that does not bear fruit He takes away; and every branch that bears fruit He prunes, that it may bear more fruit" John 15:1-2.

You must bear fruit so that God can be glorified through you.

The picture below shows some examples of how your life can be productive. You must belong to one area or the other in the Body of Christ.

(The Mini Poster 'Where Do You Belong in The Body of Christ' is available for free download at: www.christytolaministries.org/edificationposter.html):

Where Do You Belong In The Body Of Christ?

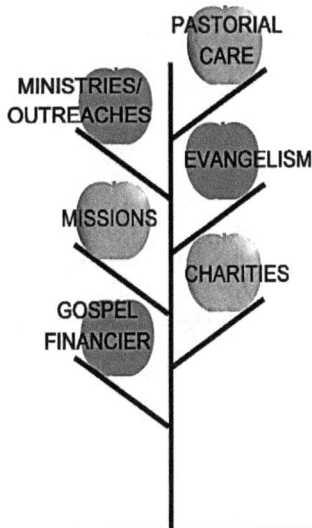

PASTORIAL CARE

MINISTRIES/ OUTREACHES

EVANGELISM

MISSIONS

CHARITIES

GOSPEL FINANCIER

"By this My Father is glorified, that you bear much fruit; so you will be My disciples"
John 15:8 (NKJV).

© 2004 Christy Tola
christytolaministries.org

Are You Physically Disabled?

Your disability does not mean that God has no purpose for your life. Despite your current state, you can still do some things for the Kingdom of God. He preserved your life for a reason till today. Ask Him to reveal your divine purpose to you during your prayers.

(There's a Guide at the End of this Book *'Tips for Hearing Clearly from God.'* It will improve your knowledge about hearing from God).

4

Conclusion

Reading the Scriptures, praising, worshipping, and praying to God, are mandatory for all Christians. We must always create the atmosphere of His Presence. This is for our protection and everything that belong to us. This will also aid our success in life.

Once we have accepted Jesus Christ as our Lord and Savior, we have entered into a relationship with God. We will be able to draw Him closer to us when we begin to praise, worship and pray to Him. An important point to note from our key Scripture is that the donkey and his master both live in the same place;

*"The Ox knows its Owner
And the donkey its Master's crib..."* Isaiah 1:3.

We are God's Temple. When we fellowship with Him consistently, His Presence will be in and around us all the time.

27

"But You are holy,
Enthroned in the praises of Israel" Psalm 22:3.

Are You in a Backslidden State?

A Christian who does not seek God consistently will soon revert back to his or her old sinful ways. This is called backsliding.

"For if, after they have escaped the pollutions of the world through the knowledge of the Lord and Savior Jesus Christ, they are again entangled in them and overcome, the latter end is worse for them than the beginning.
For it would have been better for them not to have known the way of righteousness, than having known it, to turn from the holy commandment delivered to them.
But it has happened to them according to the true proverb: "A dog returns to his own vomit," and, "a sow, having washed, to her wallowing in the mire"
2 Peter 2:20-22.

If you have recently accepted Jesus Christ as your Lord and Savior, it's my prayer that this will not happen to you. But, if you're in such state at the moment, you can still 'return home'. God is waiting for you.

> *"I will heal their backsliding,*
> *I will love them freely,*
> *For My anger has turned away from him"*
> Hosea 14:4 (NKJV).

Please say the Prayer of re-dedication below:

> *"I will arise and go to my father, and will say to him,*
> *"Father, I have sinned against heaven and before you"*
> *Luke 15:18.*

Heavenly Father,
Please forgive me. I repent and want to come back to
you. Thank You Jesus for being my Lord and Savior. Let
the Holy Spirit come and help me and reveal my Divine
Purpose to me. In Jesus name. Amen.

It's important to stay close to your Source and to create the atmosphere of worship continuously in your life. This is to prevent you from losing God's Presence, that is supposed to protect and restore or help you, when you're about to go astray. You are also likely to be subjected to demonic attacks or infestations, if you have no Anointing around you.

You must also note this; if you do not praise and worship God consistently, you will make it almost impossible for Him to help you in times of need. Praise and worship atmosphere is God's 'Clinic 'where He attends to His 'Patients', and we are His 'Patients'. We always have one situation or the other requiring His divine assistance. Many Christians sustain spiritual injuries that require spiritual surgery. This can only be fixed in the atmosphere of worship.

We will be allowing God to fight our battles anytime we praise Him. If you are always having nightmares or other spiritual afflictions, engage yourself more in intense praise, but must be accompanied by worship. Also, if your heart has been broken by someone recently, it can be mended during worship. God wants to fill the void in your life. Allow Him.

Furthermore, worship atmosphere creates God's divine favor around us. We need His favor as we deal with people and situations every day of our life. For example, if you are going for a job interview, you need the favor of God in the sight of those that will be interviewing you. When you worship before going for the job interview, God's divine favor and Presence will be around you. Obtaining the job is guaranteed if it's in accordance to His will for you.

Your breakthrough for everything in life is in the Presence of God. Make it a habit to worship Him every day of your life. Let the world see the fruit that comes with giving your life to Jesus Christ so that God can be glorified through you.

(If you are a new Christian, there are many Praise and Worship Music on YouTube and iTunes. Make good use of them).

Please Remember These Important Points:

The reading of the Scriptures must be done day and night, or as often as time permits you. Don't forget to worship or sing immediately after reading and you should also pray all the time and not only when you need God's help.

"Pray without ceasing" 1 Thessalonians 5:17.

Always take note of some relevant Scriptures during your Daily Devotion and write some on small/index cards. Take them with you as you go about your daily activities and meditate on them to protect your mind. Make effort to memorize some of them too. You never know when you will be in a spiritual warfare situation and may need some for your protection. Learn to use the Scriptures to speak (by faith) to challenging situations.

Here are some examples of some Scriptures for meditation and memorization:

Scriptures for Meditation

"Then the glory of the LORD went up from the cherub, and paused over the threshold of the temple; and the house was filled with the cloud, and the court was full of the brightness of the LORD's glory" Ezekiel 10:4.

"Blessed is the man
Who walks not in the counsel of the ungodly,
Nor stands in the path of sinners,
Nor sits in the seat of the scornful;
But his delight is in the law of the LORD,
And in His law he meditates day and night"
Psalm 1:1-2.

"May the LORD answer you in the day of trouble;
May the name of the God of Jacob defend you;
May He send you help from the sanctuary,
And strengthen you out of Zion" Psalm 20:1-2.

"He opened the rock, and water gushed out;
It ran in the dry places like a river" Psalm 105:41.

"...When he brings out his own sheep, he goes before
them; and the sheep follow him, for they know his voice.
Yet they will by no means follow a stranger, but will flee
from him, for they do not know the voice of strangers"
John 10:4-5.

"Brethren, I do not count myself to have apprehended;
but one thing I do, forgetting those things which are
behind and reaching forward to those things which are
ahead, I press toward the goal for the prize of the
upward call of God in Christ Jesus"
Philippians 3:13-14.

Scriptures for Memorization:

"...Prophesy to these bones, and say to them, 'O dry
bones, hear the word of the LORD! Thus says the Lord

GOD to these bones: "Surely I will cause breath to enter into you, and you shall live" Ezekiel 37:4-5.

"No weapon formed against you shall prosper,
And every tongue which rises against you in judgment
You shall condemn.

"He permitted no one to do them wrong;
Yes, He rebuked kings for their sakes,
Saying, "Do not touch My anointed ones,
And do My prophets no harm" Psalm 105:14-15.

"That He would grant you, according to the riches of His glory, to be strengthened with might through His Spirit in the inner man" Ephesians 3:16.

"For I,' says the LORD, 'will be a wall of fire all around her, and I will be the glory in her midst'" Zechariah 2:5.

You can utilize the blank pages at the back of this book to record some important Scriptures if you have no Scripture Journal at the moment. I will advise you to purchase one as soon as possible.

Spiritual Guides for Hearing from God

(It's important that you accept Jesus Christ as your Lord and Savior before using the Guides below. Please see Page 4 for details)

Guide for Hearing Clearly from God:

1. Read some Chapters of the Book of Psalm

2. Read 1 Samuel 3:1-10 and John 10:3-5

3. Please say the following Scriptures (saying them several times is better as Scriptures are Seed):

"In all your ways acknowledge Him,
And He shall direct your paths"
Proverbs 3:6.

"I will instruct you and teach you in the way you should go; I will guide you with My eye"
Psalm 32:8.

"My soul wait silently for God alone,
For my expectation is from Him" Psalm 62:5.

"Oh, send out Your light and Your truth!
Let them lead me..." Psalm 43:3.

4. Worship God with your favorite Gospel Music or sing songs of adoration to Him

(I will recommend 'God is Here' worship music by Martha Munizzi on YouTube. The Lyrics goes with your prayer request)

5. Pray as you're led by the Holy Spirit

6. Ask God your questions.

Important Information:

i.   Always keep a notepad and pen with you and write down the Instructions that you will receive from God. He can speak when you least expected and in any form that He chooses-Dream, Vision, Intuition or Verbal. We are made differently and only God knows the best method that is suitable for each person. He can also send someone to give you instructions. You must act on the Divine Instruction that you will receive immediately.

ii. If you do not know your divine purpose or you need God's guidance about those that you're currently dating, ask simply as if you are speaking to your best friend. Ask God any question and expect a response. You will be surprised!

iii. Also, try to avoid over-eating, especially when it's close to your bedtime. If you're fond of eating before your bed-time, substitute food with fruits. Try your best to prevent flesh from interfering with your spiritual life.

iv. In addition to the above, you'll need to continuously listen to Psalms, Praise and Worship Music on audio, to maintain the atmosphere of God's Presence around you. You can also sing if you have no access to a media player.

(Curled from 'Get Cleansed and Fill Your Lamp With Oil' by Christy Tola. It's available at amazon.com).

Note for Scriptures

Note for Scriptures

Note for Scriptures

Note for Scriptures

Note for Scriptures

Note for Scriptures

Note for Scriptures

Note for Scriptures

Note for Scriptures

Note for Scriptures

Note for Scriptures

Contact Details:

Christy Tola Arts & Books
P O Box 4243
Oak Park
IL 60304. USA.

Email: contact@tolabooks.com

More information about Pastor Christy Tola @
christytolaministries.org.

Facebook: Facebook.com/Christytolaministries

Youtube: Christy Tola Ministries

Instagram: Christy Tola

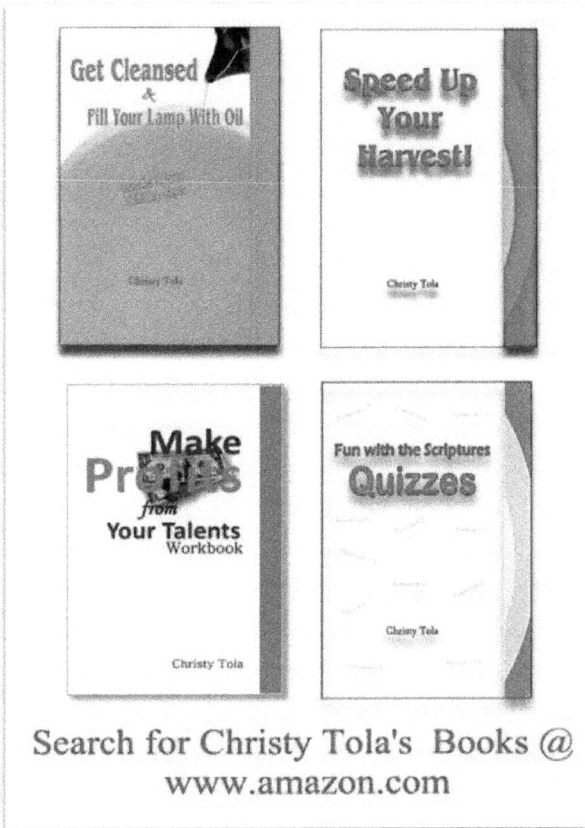

Search for Christy Tola's Books @
www.amazon.com

The Paperback Edition of 'Get Cleansed and Fill Your Lamp With Oil' and other Books by Christy Tola are now available at Amazon.com and other leading Bookstores.

www.ingramcontent.com/pod-product-compliance
Lightning Source LLC
Chambersburg PA
CBHW060622030426
42337CB00018B/3154